CAPSID
A Love Song

Joseph Osmundson

CAPSID
A Love Song

Joseph Osmundson

Indolent Books

Book design & interior illustrations: kd diamond
Cover art: kd diamond

Published by Indolent Books,
an imprint of Indolent Enterprises, LLC

www.indolentbooks.com
Brooklyn, New York

ISBN: 978-1-945023-03-3

FIGURES

The first time I tested positive for HIV, I was 23. I rode the bus north to the free clinic on 114th and 2nd Avenue in East Harlem. It was the closest one to where I lived and worked. I had a busy day and had slipped out between meetings and experiments.

I knew I was HIV negative. I was getting tested because it was the responsible thing to do—part of the story I told myself then. Because I knew the answer already, I traveled on my own. The building looked and smelled like an old elementary school: worn linoleum and soiled white walls covered in educational posters. I signed in. I checked a box: HIV Test Only. I remember the receptionist being friendly. She asked if I wanted an anonymous test. I said yes, but I had already written my name, and she had already put it in the computer. I could start the process over: leave the room, go back to the waiting room, sit in a chair, get a new number and a new form. Wait again. She asked if I had any reason to believe I was positive, or at risk. I had no reason. I had been safe. How many sexual partners have you had since your last test? One. One? One. And you've always used a condom? We have been safe. She smiled at me. We moved forward.

Getting tested is a story of waiting. They did not even prick my finger; they rubbed my gums. I waited. I had brought my laptop to do work. I had just solved my first protein structure, and I was in the process of building molecules into space. I was studying a viral protein. The waiting room was empty. It was summer, and it was warm; I remember sweating as my leg bounced up and down nervously. I was trying so hard to focus on work, on the atoms of a protein molecule in space, and never quite succeeded. Horror stories looked down at me from the posters on the walls. I waited.

A different woman called my number (nine) and pointed me into a private room. The woman was short and wide, and I remember her with a pug face, cruel and sneering. This is likely a detail added after the fact, something I needed in order to move on. She asked me to sit. The chair was cold metal, and the A/C blew cold against my leg. She asked my name. She double-checked my number. Nine. The room was small, longer than it was wide, and the woman sat at an old metal desk staring at an out-of-date computer monitor. The desk and the monitor and the woman seemed to fill the space. She told me that I was a preliminary positive. Preliminary positive. I took a breath. I did not cry. I knew it was wrong. I had been safe.

She asked if I was OK, but she was cold, all professional distance. Like she had just told me that I had stubbed a toe or sprained an ankle, something that would heal all on its own. My hands shook, but I did not cry. I knew I was fine. They pricked my finger. A second rapid test. They would send my blood work in. It would take a week.

And so I waited again, another 30 minutes for the second rapid test. I sat alone. I texted my friends, only the gay ones, and only the ones in New York. They sent hugs. They offered to come up. I remember thinking that if the second test came back positive, I would be positive, no doubt. I had not yet considered that as a possibility.

I was a false-positive that day. I took the bus back downtown and met a friend inside a restaurant near our campus for lunch. It was dark and empty inside even though it was near midday. He offered a hug while sitting on a bench with his back against the wall. I tried to open my mouth, but I just started to cry. I put my body down on that bench, behind his back. He leaned forward, his arm resting on my leg. I was still scared. I didn't want my third test to be positive. To end up on the wrong side of a statistic.

I had to wait a week for the third test results to come back. I tried to put it out of my mind. I went back to work. I woke up and walked to lab. I sat at my desk planning cloning strategies, cutting DNA sequences and splicing them back together. I read journal articles on the viruses that I studied then, viruses that only infect bacteria, killing them. I drank too much coffee and tried hard not to think. I flew to Chicago to sit in a windowless room, wider than it was long, in a particle accelerator shooting my viral protein with high-energy X-rays in an attempt to unveil its secrets.

When I returned to New York City, I traveled back to East Harlem and got the results. I became an HIV-negative man once again. For years, and even today, my hands shake when I walk into a free NYC clinic, when the smell of cheap sanitizing solutions and air freshener fighting against the musty building hits me hard, and my muscles remember and begin to move, involuntary.

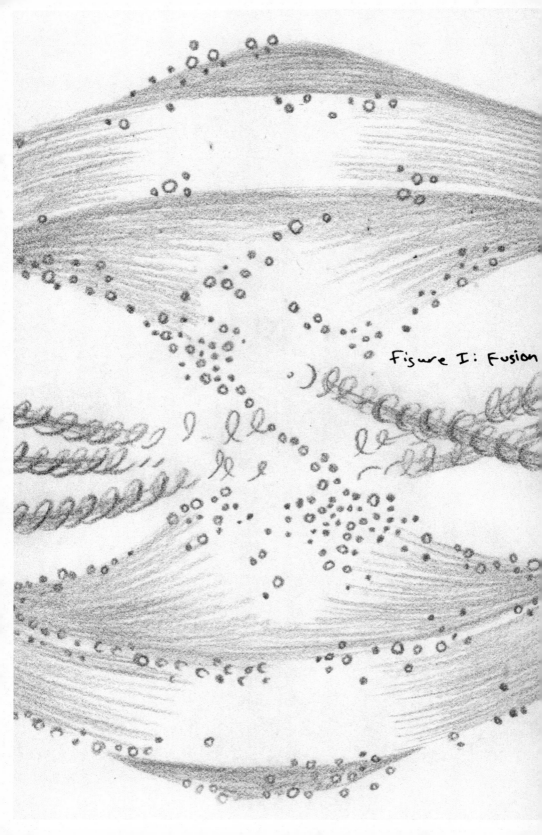

Figure I: Fusion

I. Fusion

Membranes meet, my outside and yours. My cell is an ocean, a wide fluid mosaic; your particle, a weather balloon, round, packed with thorns and spikes. You bounce off me, the two of us still distinct, the two of us still separate. Our membranes aren't enough, mine and yours; we need to find each other. A receptor. A mate.

Membranes repel, but you know that. It takes work to make two things into one, to dump your contents into my ocean. Your proteins meet mine, charges matching, fitting like a glove. Then everything starts to change. You change. Fusion requires work.

But you do the work, don't you? Swing yourself open, stick your thorns and spikes into me for good. One spike, gp120, unfurls another, gp41. You pull us close, membranes touching, your outside and my outside closer now and closer now, and finally you are more than bound. We are two halves, almost one. You wait, you wait. Our membranes shimmer into onto another. My ocean, your balloon, and I am open to you, I am open and wider and wider, the work is done, all downhill from here.

And you release it, your ordered capsid, your self-assembled self. You release it into me.

Even before I understood that I wanted to sleep with men, I knew that sex could be death. I am a child of the '90s. I saw the pictures on TV. It was always on TV, and never in my life. It was always them, not us. It was hidden, though, and could get you at any time. Pleasure was never safe, only safer. Today, tonight, when I go home, when I fuck, HIV will sit in the back of my brain, a thought not molded into stone, inchoate but present. Present, just there. Is this the time?

But Jesse wasn't like me. He was a child of the '90s too, but maybe just less neurotic, more well-adjusted, less scared. Jesse thinks—he knows—that he is only HIV negative because he is a top. He says it, and he knows it is not true. It is a myth and a dangerous one. Yet it is an explanation that fits, and that feels fair, more so perhaps than the truth.

He did not worry until it hurt to piss. He did not worry until the boy, together for four years and monogamous for three, broke down. Confessed. He did not worry until doctors. He did not worry until results. He tried to forget the boyfriend sex, the waking up between night and morning and just needing to have each other. He had even bottomed, even though it hurt, because he realized it only hurt at first.

He says I am only negative because I am a top. We are in his car driving in Washington, D.C. It is summer, windows down, Aretha on the speakers, and we are talking about HIV and how it seems to be everywhere in our lives. Jesse's boy had only topped him twice, three times. He says that's how I stayed safe, accidentally. He says I should have it already, and I'm lucky not to, and if I ever do get it, I will have had a few extra years, free. Jesse and his boy stayed together a year after one diagnosis and one dodged bullet. They lived in that same apartment. They talked about viral loads. They were two bodies moving apart slowly, week by week, sitting farther from each other on the couch with the TV filling their silence. They talked about drugs, HAART. They stopped talking much at all.

We are alive, positive and negative and unknown and undetectable, we are alive today, and we will be tomorrow if tomorrow we are granted. We are alive thanks to the stories we tell. He said I am only negative because I am a top. We are alive because of the words we speak into silence.

Figure II: Retrotransposition

II. Retrotransposition

You take yourself apart to put yourself back together. Destruction is the first step. Your capsid, yourself, will be undone. Those repeating copies of six, of ten, of two, a lattice like a crystal, a patchwork like a soccer ball but longer, like a football made to spiral, that capsid you built so carefully, it falls apart like an old building, brick by brick. You use me to do it. How else would you know that you're home, that you're safe, that we are together?

And then you are naked. RNA, mutable, degradable. Your two-prime hydroxyl make you unstable; you are vulnerable to intramolecular attack. You have become the smallest version of yourself, nothing but the blueprints to make you rise again days later from the ashes.

Copying yourself is the first requisite. But you need me; you can't do this alone. You make your new self from me. You make mistakes. You copy your genes the same way I do, block by block, requiring work, bases moving against bases to test for their partner, their mate. But you make mistakes, and your mistakes will kill you and save you. You copy your RNA, unstructured, into that ordered double helix, DNA, so famous, so permanent.

Years ago now. The first time I found his profile online, I cried into the night. I was drunk, and he was downtown. Working. But then I had to wonder if that was true. The picture was him, chest and stomach: I knew that body anywhere, I had watched it above me so many times as he opened me wide and carried me past myself. The words, too, were him, unmistakable. Him him him. Looking for: one-on-one sex; threesomes/group sex. Just seeing what's out there. No old guys.

We fought, but I relented. He needed the chase. He needed that validation. He was not sleeping with those boys. He was only sleeping with me. He just needed the chase. The validation.

We had stopped using condoms after two negative tests. Or: We started fucking raw after two negative tests. He showed me the piece of paper with his name, signed by the doctor. Negative. That I could not control his sex was part of it. That he had a history of back rooms and bathhouses was a part of it. That he might let me join him there sometimes, in the bathhouses and back rooms, was part of it.

I can speak of the parts but I cannot explain the whole. I wanted him in a new way. I was not young when we met. I wanted the smell of him. I thought he was so beautiful that he would never talk to me. Until he did. I thought he was so beautiful that he would never kiss me. Until he did. I thought a boy like that would never want to fuck me. But then he did. He always wanted to be clean, but sometimes, when he was feeling generous, he would agree not to shower before I sucked his dick. I liked how he smelled, tasted. Funky, but perfect. Ripe. That was him, that was us. I was not a bottom, but he was mostly a top. It probably had helped keep him safe. I had never been a bottom before, not consistently. Our sex smelled like clean sheets and amyl nitrite. It tasted like a pillow and a bitten lip. Like blood. It felt rare and fragile and carefully made. It was raw. We never did go to a sex club, did we? We never did fuck in back rooms, not together.

We fucked raw for years, believing in our own monogamy, trusting in each other's health. I got tested, yes, it was the responsible thing to do, but now it was with the worry of that raw sex eating away at my faith. I sat and my leg bounced nervously, uncontrollably, and I carried a deep lump in my throat. Negative: I was still fine.

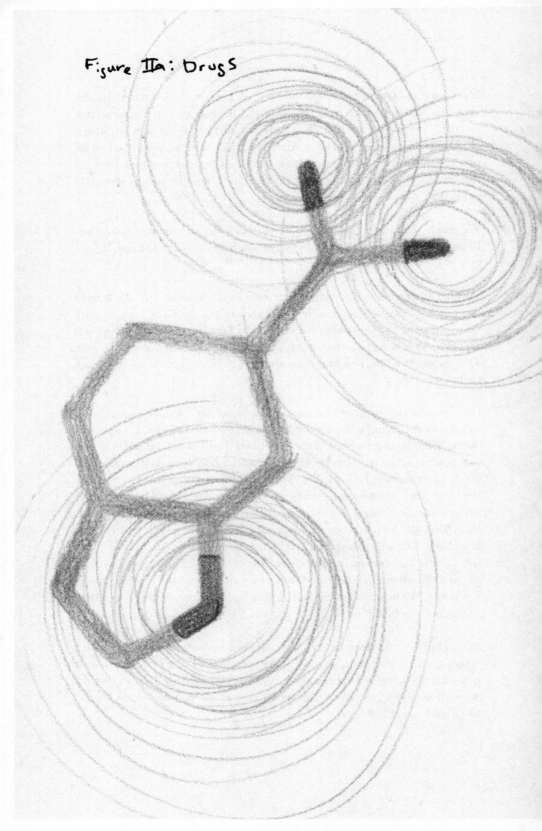

Figure IIa: Drugs

IIa. Drugs/Small molecule inhibitors

And this is where the war begins. This is where I can rid myself of you, or at least keep you quiet, mute. I will gather my troops against you. 3TC. We will build a barrier, a wall, and you will lay siege, and your power is in numbers, ever growing, ever changing. Tenofovir. They bind to your enzymes, these soldiers, these drugs, fitting into your proteins like a key, and they stop you from copying yourself. But you make mistakes. That is your power, to change, to mutate, to make a lock that my soldiers cannot bind. Together these drugs lower your chances of escape, small but present, until they are zero. Abacavir. One one-thousandth. Indinavir. One one-thousandth times one one-thousanth. Ten to the minus six. Didanosine. Ten to the minus six times one one-thousandth. Ten to the minus nine. And you can't copy yourself enough. You cannot escape. Lamivudine. The barriers. Etravirine. The walls.

We made these soldiers. We built them together. They are made of our dead. They speak for the gone. We built them together, bodies and industry; capital and ash; activists and artists and scientists and doctors pushing and dying and pushing and dying. To me the drugs are the dead, the gone. They are made of the black bags we were stuffed inside. They are made of the body shakes and the bloody tears we had to cry alone. They can save me now. They have saved so many, stopped you so many times from brining death, certain death. For decades now, they have kept us out of our own black garbage bags. Cobicistat. Norvir. They are made of all things holy: cum and piss and sweat; industry and capital; the bodies of the gone, and the names of the dead.

We all talk, my friends and I, about the silence, the loneliness. The fear of getting the virus, the stigma of having it, how difficult it is to come out, another coming out, worse than the first. But we know we have to do it; we aren't allowed, according to the law, to have sex without stating our status. Confirming our danger. Placing the risk solidly there, understood by all partners: a choice to make.

We talk about the silence, my friends and I, and we are all tired. We share stories, but it is hard to share them here, to put the words down in black and white. They say yes, they want to talk on the record, but then they avoid the conversation, knowing that the words will, this time, be written for all to see. We are all tired of the silence, but I get it: No one wants the silence broken across their own back. No one wants their name on a list. Tragic HIV story. Slut. Irresponsible, should have known better. I wonder how he got it. I wonder from whom. A sex party, probably; a raw hookup, online.

Of course there are stories I could tell, stories that are anonymous enough, untraceable. Like invitations to dinners, to drinks, that fall off after one word is spoken: positive. Friends that fall off without falling out. It is hard to say what the reason is, but the suspicions are probably correct, the timing too neat to be coincidental. Like the fear of ending up alone. Like getting dumped when he finally told the boy, three dates in but before anything more than a kiss, that word: positive. Like wondering how much sex is too much before one must, legally or ethically, disclose. A blow job? What if I only bottom? What if it's always safe? What if I am undetectable? Like knowing without having to count exactly how many people know your full truth. Positive: seven. Then mom, dad: nine. Like living in a closet within a closet where it is easier sometimes to come out (positive) to a boy you just met online than to a best friend of ten years, planning dinner after dinner to tell them, finally tell them, but the words always choke, punch, and the tears well up, and it is easier, always easier, to turn the conversation back to school and work and TV and books. Like worrying about getting 800 calories before noon in order to be able to take that pill, the one that keeps you alive.

Stories stories. Like the time I was out drinking and dancing with friends at one of the Hell's Kitchen bars, all pop remixes and cheap drinks. I felt like I was surrounded by 22-year-olds, which is to say that I felt old, but I was there with my old friends and we were dancing and laughing and drunk enough to feel free but not drunk enough to fight. Across the dance floor, across the endless number of faces, blurring into one another with motion, one face was frozen with recognition. I smiled wide. I loved these chance encounters, running into a friend after three attempted dinner dates. I was happy to see James, and he seemed happy to see me. We hugged tight, and he lifted my feet off the ground, spun my body around in the middle of the dance floor, boys moving out of the way of our two bodies, turning in circles. We launched into our three-minute life summaries, catching up before both of our friends pulled us apart again. He was talking fast, talking about teaching, about relationships. Then he said it. Oh yeah and I am finally positive and I am so happy about it. And the new job is busy, but good, rewarding. It took a moment to register, the words replaying in my mind. Could he have said that? Here? Now? Just like that? Positive, and on to the next topic? And he is happy about it? I thought about it for days; I questioned all my assumptions, my own hypochondria, my own fear. I know the image we have of bug chasers, abused or sad men who hate themselves. James was a doctor: fit, handsome, smart, talented. He cured people, made them healthy again. And he was positive. Like so many others. But happy about it and willing to break the silence and tell his story to the world, or at least to me, there, drunk, dizzy, in the middle of a sea of dancing 22 year olds.

Stories stories. Like a friend from college who does not know if she is positive or negative. The numbers tell us this is not just an epidemic of young gay men. Women are getting it too, straight women, and straight men. Korina is living in the months between unprotected sex and a definitive test. She has a hard time sleeping at night, not knowing. The man was her ex, and he had cheated when they were together, over and over, but she just could not quite get rid of him. There was just something about him, how he made her feel, how he could make her feel, in a moment, like she was the only girl that mattered, that the others were just noise. She let herself be reckless with him, and when he came back into her life (begging, begging) she let herself be reckless again. It was safe at first, protected, but he promised he had only been safe with other girls since they ended, and that those girls didn't mean shit, and that they didn't feel like this. Sometime in the night she relented, and now she is living in the months between. She does not want to get tested yet; she wants to wait. She does not have the time to waste sitting over and over in doctor's offices or free clinics. She cannot take it emotionally, a negative test but with an asterisk. She wants to go once and have it be done with. She only wants the test once it can be definitive. Either way he is out of her life. Either way she is free.

I tell these stories with permission because none of the details would open that second closet door: positive. Silence remains necessary at times for survival.

The full truth is only allowed to exist between the lines. In the details generic enough to be safe. In the pauses. In the blank spaces, the made-up bits.

Figure III: Integration

III. Integration

This is where we become one: not my cell and your particle, but my molecules become yours become mine become yours. This is our point of no return. You have made yourself into something more like me already. Copied your molecules, your RNA into my permanence: DNA. But we are still two molecules. But then you again cut yourself to survive. Cleave off your ends. And then you use these ends. To put yourself in me. You cut me open, don't you? You break my bonds, cleave me open to put yourself inside. You become me, your helix and my helix one extended chain. You are my molecule, now and forever. You are my DNA, one and the same. Now and forever. One and the same.

It's the early 1990s. I do not remember the ads on TV, but I know they existed. I was born in 1983, and I remember the Berlin Wall falling. I was sitting in front of the TV on the floor with my mom and dad behind me. I somehow knew it was a big moment, an important moment, something to remember. Perhaps it was the silence in my house, so rare. I was the youngest, and everyone else was staring, rapt, at the TV.

I do not have a moment with HIV. I do not remember specific ads, but I know that they were there. MTV, for sure, but elsewhere too. Use condoms. HIV kills. You don't catch it by hugging. Use condoms. AIDS kills. You can't catch it by sharing a Coke. I looked back to inform my memory. I looked into the digital archive that is the internet. There were ads, specials. Raps, commercials. People black and white and always straight, in the ads, always straight from what I remember and from what I see now. Reminding us.

But even for gay men and even in urban centers, living through the 1990s meant that HIV and sex were interconnected, one and the same. Half of us gay men have HIV in our minds when we're having sex. Sex is never just sex; it is safe sex, safer sex, unsafe sex. It is always qualified. I am always thinking about it. I am not alone. It is a product of our time, of our childhood, of our lives.

One memory sticks out. I am 12, I must be. If I am 12, it is 1995. My sister is four years older than I am. She is 16. My parents had the master bedroom in our house, their own room with an attached bathroom that my sister and I could scramble into only in case of emergency. My parents had the only comfortable bed, but we were not allowed to linger on it. They needed their sanctuary. It is the afternoon and therefore it is either the weekend or during the summer. I think it is summer because the light coming in from the window, looking west, is summer light: warm, peaceful, inviting. I am lying on the bed, my small frame wrapped into itself, and my sister is there too, next to me, but we do not touch. My mom sits on the side of the bed, her feet on the floor. She faces west.

We talk about sex. I am 12. My voice is still high. I have not yet attempted to jerk off. I know nothing about that type of pleasure. This is not the talk. I know where babies come from. When I was little we were poor. My mom taught Lamaze classes in the evenings for extra money. Because my father worked too, I would go and sit in the back of my mother's Lamaze classes so that they did not have to pay for a babysitter. By the time I was 12 I had sat through the class so many times that I became a teaching assistant. On evenings when a mother-to-be's partner could not make it to class, I would sit by her side and practice breathing with her. I would rub her back and look into her eyes as my own mother walked around the room checking in with each couple.

We are, the three of us, on my parents' bed in my parents' room. My mom talks about protection. About being safe. My mom says that it's beautiful, but you have to be safe. You can get sick. It can kill you. I am confused. If it is so dangerous, why do we do it? What could feel so good that you would do it even if it would kill you? I say I'm not going to have sex, ever. Because why would I if it could kill you? Why would I if it is so unsafe? Why would I have sex if protection is so important? Why risk my life? I am lying down, remember, and my mom is looking down at me. I lean my head back to look up at her. She is smiling, wide. Well, she says, it is pleasurable. And it expresses love. It's beautiful. You just have to be safe. AIDS kills. You can't catch it by sharing a Coke.

I could not say when it happened, if it happened, which of the nights of all those nights it happened. I want to imagine that it was an afternoon in the summer. We came home from walking around Soho, window-shopping because we were both too poor to buy, holding hands in public, laughing about a dumb commercial we saw on TV that morning while we sat and ate the eggs and bacon and pancakes that I made while he cleaned his room. We came home that afternoon and I wanted him so badly, I had been waiting all morning to feel his chest on me. I had to pry myself out of bed those days. Leaving his body, naked, to face the day was too much to bear. We came home that Sunday afternoon in summer, and I followed him back down the hallway to his room and shut the door behind us. It startled him. He turned around. I was already on my knees. I pushed his body back onto the bed, he turned me over, we both pulled off the shorts and tank tops we had been wearing. His head moved down my body, and I was in his mouth, full. The light came in through his blinds, lines of light and dark alternating diagonally across his bed, his sheets, blue, and his body and mine. His bed was so much more comfortable than mine. I was on my back and in his mouth, and I looked at the light falling on his shoulders, and I felt nothing but pleasure, and I was not worrying about anything, not work, not words. You couldn't hear the street noise from his room—it was quiet, rare in this city. He turned me over. I was lying on my chest and his chest was on my back, thick with that hair, and it was hot, it was summer, so he felt wet and I felt wet, the air felt wet, and when a rare breeze came in through the window it made us both shiver. I know because I could feel him shiver too. I pushed back into him and he pushed forward into me.

That day we did not clean up. We fell asleep in our sweat, lines of light cutting our bodies diagonally, until it was time to make dinner. If it happened, that is the day that I choose.

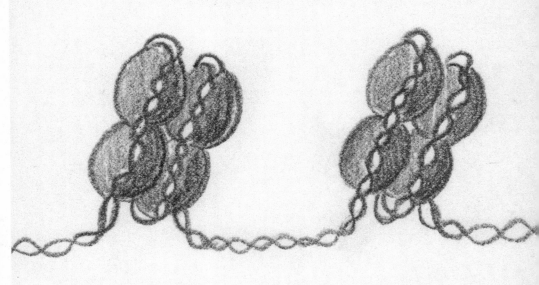

Figure IV: Latency

IV. Latency

Now that we are one, the same, you can hide in me. Or with me. My body's defenses have a memory, and they will carry you in them, for always. You knew right where to attack, didn't you, cutting down the part of myself that I need to fight, to fight you, to fight others, other diseases, other viruses, our own cancers. Even with my drugs, fighting to keep you quiet, you refuse to be killed, to be gone. You turn yourself off, quiet your genes, hide your needs, to fight another day. For when my soldiers are no longer a part of my diet. For when my defenses fall. You sit and lie in wait. You are me but you will hide until the day my soldiers are not present to fight, until that day, and perhaps before, you will wait. You will reemerge.

I am a scientist writing about HIV, and I am finally going to do the expected. I am going to talk about numbers. After years of HAART therapy, multidrug cocktails, there has been movement on a cure. There was the Berlin patient, cured by his cancer, the loss and rebirth of his immune system from a donor resistant to viral fusion. There is Truvada, the option to have drugs, soldiers coursing through the body, fighting off future infection, defending against the very idea of HIV. And now even more news, news that reminds me of a story. Years ago I was walking with a friend at the gay beach in NYC, in the Rockaways. The beach itself was nothing special, a patch of sand, dirty, the Atlantic, dirty, but it was covered with our people, gay boys and gay girls. I was walking down to the end of the beach, just my feet in the water because it was still early in the summer and the water was cold. We were talking about hookups. My friend said that he was not afraid of sleeping with a man with HIV. If he knew he had it, and if he was on drugs, it was safer than sleeping with a random, a boy he did not trust, that did not know he had it. In that moment, a lump grew in my throat, and I looked at this friend with pity. How could he be so reckless, so irresponsible? But this past summer he was proved right: Undetectable men, the ones who know their status, the ones controlling the infection with drugs, are not passing on their infections, even when they have unprotected sex. They are safe.

More numbers: HIV has been present in my life because I live in New York City (among the U.S. cities with the highest rates of infection). HIV has been present in my life because I sleep with men. I am gay. Or queer. Or, since we are talking about HIV, I am a MSM: a man who has sex with men. We know that more than two-thirds of new HIV cases are found in MSM, but we are classified as only 2 percent of the population. HIV has been present in my life because I am relatively young and we know that there has been a spike in new HIV infections among younger gay men in particular. HIV has been present in my life because HIV has always touched those who live on our margins: gay people, poor people, people of color, people in prison, and these are my people, my family, my life. We know the statistics. We were born into the danger. We know that sex can kill. And yet, we are the newly infected. We see people living with. Living in spite of. Living. We are tired of being afraid of sex, of bodies. All people have affairs. All human bodies know disease. All bodies take risks. It is just that some of us pay more dearly for ours.

But enough. We know about the numbers already anyway, and I am not sure that they teach us much in the moments after our clothes come off. Because it is not about numbers, is it? We talk about it as though it were numbers and drugs, a problem and a solution, simple epidemiology. But no, it is about pleasure and bodies and sex and death and deviance and sin. That is why it was ignored for a decade. That is why we died.

Bodies fail us, don't they? They leak, they break, they give way, age, shrink, fail to perform. But bodies create our pleasure, and through our pleasure, a desire to give pleasure to other beings, other bodies. In these sought-after moments of pleasure, the rest of the world falls away, the world with its responsibilities and deadlines and disappointments and suffering. Pleasure never grows old. Orgasms never die. But it is not safe, and we know it. We have known it for almost three decades now. My whole adult life. Where can we run now? What can take away this last, final worry? How can we stop our bodies from breaking, fast with the help of a virus, or slow, the old-fashioned way, with just time and gravity, cancer waiting, heart disease in the wings, dementia sitting on our left shoulder? It will happen to us all one way or another. And where can we run? Where can we hide when not even pleasure is pure, if it ever was?

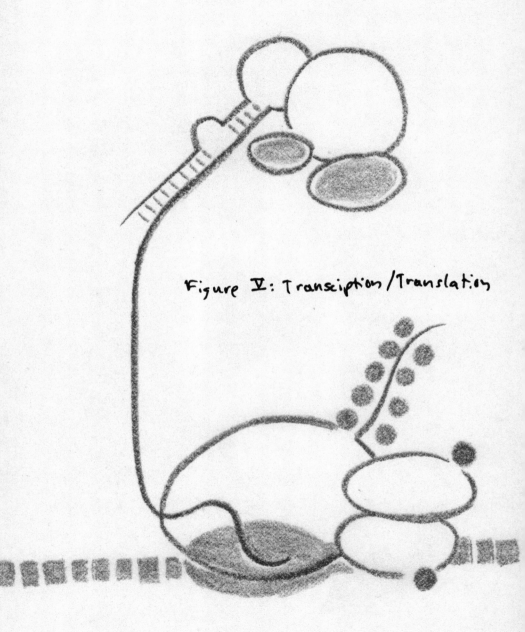

Figure IV: Transciption/Translation

V. Transcription/Translation

But you refuse to be silent for long, don't you? A week without drugs, you reemerge. I do it for you at first, you are just genes in my genes like any others, and I turn you on. You are restrained, considerate; you know this is not your house. Not yet. I only make two proteins for you, at first. Or is it for us, now? These two proteins change me, us. And they turn you on. You lose your restraint. You remember that what's mine is yours, now. You transcribe all your genes. You make proteins that carry you around me, breaking all the rules. You turn my factories into your factories, my machines into yours. You make yourself fully now, prepare for your eventual escape, your release. And I get lost in your enthusiasm, I become a tool, used at your will. I don't mind; I don't mind. Slowly, as you build yourself, you destroy me.

I am writing the end twice because neither is the end. Both ends are true. They are my story, and ours.

The month he was gone smelled like honeysuckle and tasted like gin. I felt free from his moods, his expectations. I felt free of our sex, which had become all-encompassing, unsustainable. I had been putting off my yearly checkup for three months. I was afraid, and I could not step back into a free clinic, but I was nervous about the phone call from my doctor, a life changed, not death anymore, just a new and careful life, an excuse for therapy, a longing still for sustainable connection.

I asked him to use a condom after the last time I found him online. It was a break between us, a rupture. It hurt him. We didn't fuck that afternoon, we talked and talked, made truth, broke it, made it again. Kissed slow and deep. And walked out to get dinner. It was blow jobs and jerking off for a while. Blow jobs and jerking off were hot. But we wanted to fuck, and who could blame us. We used condoms. He told me he had no profiles online. Work took him to Prague for a month. I biked home from lab.

He would say that I cheated too, and he would not be lying. He found messages, Facebook, emails, texts, messages from exes, messages from boys. Tender and emotional messages. He was never tender or emotional with any of the boys he was talking to, that much I do believe. But I was always longing for something more, and when I was hurt, which was often, I would run to someplace safe. To a boy who wanted me. He found out, and my infidelities gave him permission to feel safe in his world of Grindr, of boys ever wanting him, wanting him so badly, begging him for it, just once, looking for now. His infidelities gave me permission to feel safe in my world of boys, boys who wanted me, for my heart, for my brain, boys who wanted to be with me, who would ensure that I would not be alone, not forever.

The doctor came and went. The waiting, in my life with health insurance and primary care physicians, was done at a respectful distance. I waited for a phone call. There was no waiting room, no posters speaking worst-case scenarios into being.

I was biking, on my way to the lab, when I was released. When I got free. I had played this game before. I knew who would be calling me from an unlisted number three days after my appointment. I pulled over to listen to the message. I was standing, one foot on the sidewalk and one on my bike, the morning rush-hour traffic floating past my right shoulder, as I listened to the message. Negative. Or was the word she used normal? I was standing in the shadow of the New York Public Library, expansive, bricks and marble, stairs and gardens, on 42nd Street and 5th Avenue, with one foot on the sidewalk and one foot on my bike, traffic so close behind me that I could feel the air rush off car after car after car, when I was released. When I got free.

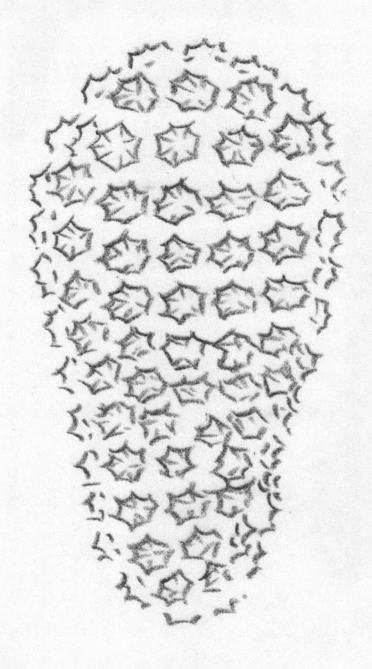

Figure II: Assembly

VI. Assembly

You have made yourself again from me; you have regained a separate identity, molecules that we can call yours, RNA and protein that belong to you apart from the bit that you stuck in me, which remains. First you cut yourself again and again, cleave your protein into its working components. You assemble. Your capsid, so ordered, repeating surfaces of perfect mirrors, hexagons meeting hexagons again and again, grows. Randomly, randomly, pieces come together, often wrong but sometimes right, often misshapen, an odd lump of clay, but sometimes that perfect oblong sphere, your capsid, yourself.

I am writing the end twice. Both ends are true. They are my story, and ours. The second time I tested positive for HIV, he was in Prague for work. The month he was gone smelled like honeysuckle and tasted like gin. I felt free from his moods, his expectations. It was spring, summer was on the horizon, showing herself but only sometimes, always unpredictable, and I chased her. I biked home from lab, through Central Park, and when it had rained during the day or night the honeysuckle bordered on overwhelming, cloyingly sweet, too much of a good thing.

When I first moved to New York, HIV was a fear that was present in my mind but not in my life. Not that I knew of, anyway. I knew positive people, but—to my knowledge—it was no one close to me. These people seemed to fit too neatly into a 1990s HIV narrative: They were older gay men who had somehow and miraculously survived the plague, who had become infected before we knew any better. That is not our story anymore, if it ever was. We are a generation of people who grew up knowing too much and trying to run from this knowledge. It is now our turn to make mistakes and to regret them, to love recklessly and without guilt, to be safe, as safe as we can.

I got the call on my way to work, biking down 5th Avenue. I knew right away: They do not ask you to come back for a consult if everything is fine. In a flash, my life changed. This time my hands did not shake. I was outside under the city sky and skyscrapers, with city smells and the humidity pushing down on me. I have to say this. It is not my fault, it is not his. Forgiveness is not mine to give or seek. It is not a death sentence. It is a call to life. It is not isolation. It is a call to connect. It is not disease. It is a call to care. I am not full of hate. I breathe in our love. It is not stigma. It is community. We are the vanguard. We refuse to budge. This is the battle. This is the war. We will live. We will love. We will fuck: dark and dirty, safe but always dangerous, with the greatest care and pleasure, sharing our bodies and spirits, sharing the best and worst of ourselves. Drink from this, all of you, this is my blood. Take this and eat it, for this is my body.

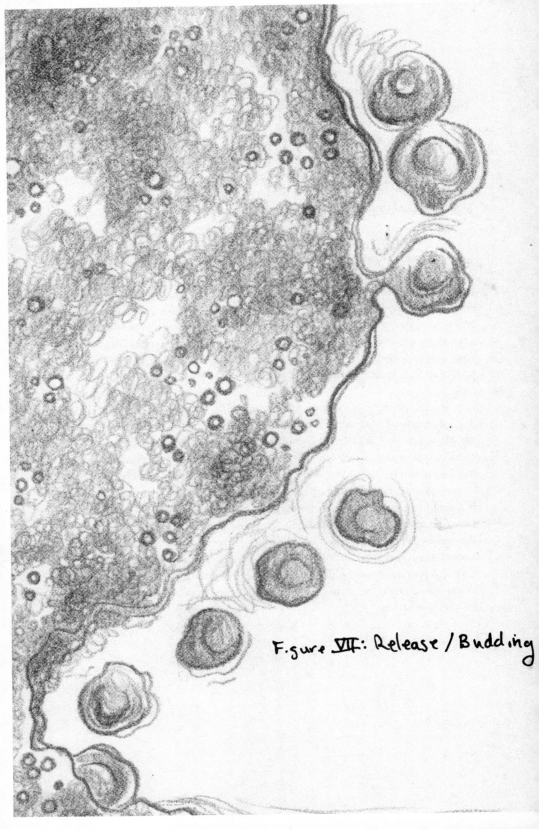

Figure VII: Release / Budding

VII. Release/Budding

We are my kind of unhappy, you and I. Twins of sorts, one and the same. Let me unfurl my capsid. Let me copy myself. Let our membranes touch again. I can't have been the only one to have felt it those months or years ago.

But I get it now. Your story is like this one. Like all stories we tell. A mix of fact and fiction. Of pleasure and pain. I cannot tell the difference between the two anymore, and so I write to fill the space. To speak into the silence we built, you and I, together.

In my life will it be possible to cut you out, to root you out, to kill the space you have taken in me while I survive, live and breathe? In my life will it be possible to transform and shape-shift? In my life will I ever forget you, or would that be like forgetting myself? Is killing you the same as killing me? Will it take a cancer, the eradication of a part of me, to undo you? And even then: In my life would I ever be able to think about something else when I cum: a flower, maybe, in the process of being born; the way his eyes flutter; the way her chest moves?

We think we see you, but we can't. That is part of our fiction and the basis for our fact. We need tools: X-rays and crystals and electrons shot against you, already dead and painted with heavy metal. I always see you like this, in black and white, an image taken decades ago: You are covered in metal and shot through with electrons. You are budding, being released, leaving my cell, circles of membrane, your capsid visible, so ordered, self-assembled. You stick to me, our membranes still one. Until you release. Until you bud. Until, inevitably, you leave me. Until you float off into my space between, outside my cells but inside my body. I write to you there. I am the war. This is my battlefield. You are there, your own self again, just budded, just released, again an oblong ball of membrane, spikes and thorns, freed of my ocean, ready to reinfect, ready to begin the cycle again with another cell, another host. Writing to you there, I remember the dead. And, with our industry, and with our activism, and with these words, an incantation, and because of the dead, because of the gone, may you leave me, may you bud, once and forever, never to return.

ACKNOWLEDGMENTS

This essay was originally published in the *Los Angeles Review of Books*.

———————————————

Thanks, first, to Michele Pridmore-Brown and Jonathan Hahn at the *Los Angeles Review of Books*, who saw something in this piece worth publishing and who were gracious and thoughtful in their edits. Then a huge thanks to the Lambda Literary Foundation, to Randall Kenan, and to all the possums. This essay was borne from my time with you all. A special thanks to Miah Jeffra, Yana Calou, David Weinstein, Chase Quinn, and Claire Atkinson, who all made this essay better than it was before. Thanks to my parents for getting upset, but not too upset, when this was published. Thanks to everyone, too, who has loved me with this in the world, and to everyone who has read it. Thanks to Katie Diamond for our collaboration, and for making me cry by putting my weird biophysical love poem to the HIV virus in images that feel as deeply as my body, my words. A final thanks to Michael Broder and Indolent Press for making this a real book.

ABOUT THE AUTHOR

Joseph Osmundson is a scientist and writer from rural Washington State. His writing has been published in the *Los Angeles Review of Books, The Los Angeles Review, Gawker, Salon, The Rumpus*, and *The Feminist Wire*, where he is an Associate Editor. He's currently a post-doctoral fellow in systems biology at NYU.

ABOUT INDOLENT BOOKS

Indolent Books is a small independent press founded in 2015 and operating in Brooklyn. Indolent was founded as a home for poets of a certain age who have done the creative work but for whatever reason (family, career, self—effacement, etc.) have not published a first collection. But we are not dogmatic about that mission: Ultimately, we publish books we like and care about, short or long, poetry or prose. We are queer owned, queer staffed, and maintain a commitment to diversity among our authors, artists, designers, developers, and other team members.

CPSIA information can be obtained
at www.ICGtesting.com
Printed in the USA
LVOW03s1216260218
567888LV00003B/558/P